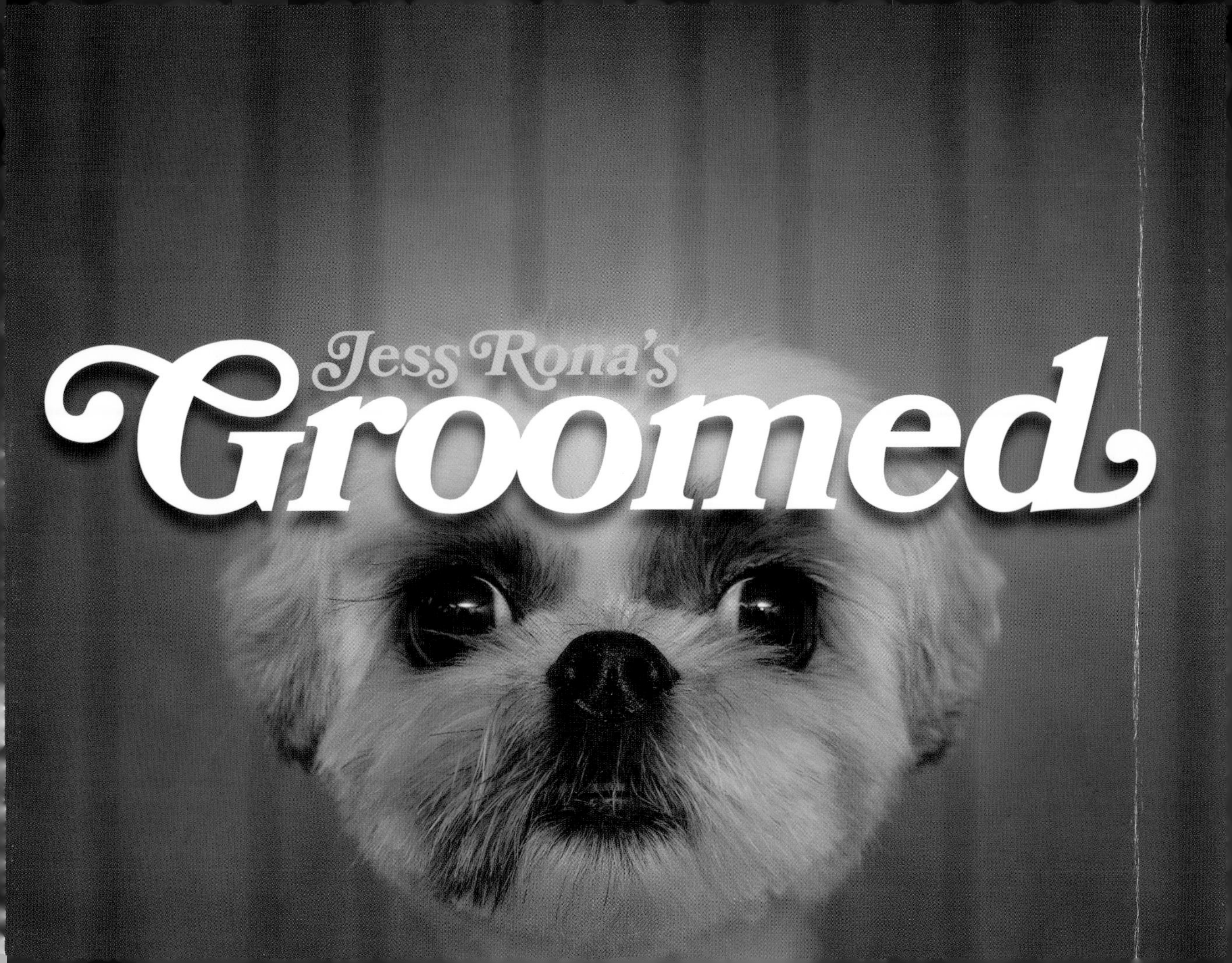
Jess Rona's
Groomed

Jess Rona's
Groomed

KNOCK
KNOCK®
VENICE, CALIFORNIA

Preface

A couple of years ago at a Mafia party, a role-playing game where people kill each other off slowly over the course of a night, I met Jess Rona. I was shyly hovering near a cheese plate when she introduced herself. I felt immediately at ease with her in a room full of strangers who were about to murder me. She told me she was an actor, a musician, and a dog groomer. As a cat person, I prepared to fake interest in the Instagram page she pulled up to show me her grooming work. But suddenly I was looking at Stella, an elegant poodle, being blow dried in slow motion while "Drunk in Love" by Beyoncé played.

I was captivated.

The wood paneling of Jess's workshop made me think of the basements of my childhood and the wonderful sets on the television show *Freaks and Geeks*. The dogs in her videos looked sad, hopeful, proud, insecure. Sometimes they seemed shy or noble, dumb or sweet. The songs that soundtracked these videos—fused with artful footage—perfectly narrated the inner turmoil, grief, and contemplative intelligence I'd assumed didn't exist in dogs. Here was Blueberry, staring into my soul while Ben Gibbard sang regretfully, "I should have given you a reason to stay." Was the look in Blueberry's eyes the same devastating one we all hoped we'd given our ex when they broke up with us?

I also loved the still shots on Jess's Instagram—simple, gorgeous photographs of dogs soaked and soaped, frozen in postures of vulnerability; the shower we've all taken when we were ruined or desperate. And of course the before-and-after shots! How could I not see each of these dogs and the results of their grooming as a major makeover success?! Each "after" photo screamed, "*Look at me now, asshole!!*" Genius. That is what I thought. THIS. IS. GENIUS.

The interior lives of animals may not be as elaborate as we like to imagine, but Jess's videos and photographs have drastically changed how I see dogs. I'd spent much of my life pigeonholing them into two simple categories: as the patrol guards of suburban backyards or the spoiled spawn of helicopter pet-parents. It was Jess's work that convinced me otherwise, which was no small feat, considering how snobbish I'd always been about dogs vs. cats. And so, when my band needed a music video for a particularly sad ballad on our latest album, we asked Jess to direct it.

It's not easy for me to admit that dogs—even ones who just stare somberly into a camera or blink in slow motion with sad-sack looks on their furry faces—are probably a better stand-in for my pain than any other animal. In real life I'm introverted and suspicious, but also curious and pleased when observed by others from a safe distance. The emotional part of me that I protect and rarely share with others is the place from which I create, and the heart from where I love. I'm coming to terms with the fact that that part of me might be more of a Border collie.

Don't tell my cats.

—Sara Keirsten Quin (of Tegan and Sara)

Introduction

You're in the shower. The hot water is beating on your back, you get lost in thoughts that pound through your head. Questions and answers swirl in your mind. Suddenly you snap out of your trance and realize you've been staring at the wall for...who knows how long. You've been thinking about your lonely, broken heart, or a life-changing decision you have to make, or what to eat for dinner. In this case, "you" are a schnauzer named Nacho, and you're miserable.

When I take a photo of a dog in the bath and they look up at me all vulnerable, I'm transported to that moment we've all had in the shower. I mean, we've *all* had that moment in the shower, right?

It's hard to believe (since I look so young), but I've been a dog groomer for seventeen years. A few years ago, I found a house in the Hollywood Hills, with epic '70s wood paneling in the garage. It was the perfect place to start a private home-grooming business, which would give me more time for auditions. (Yup, I'm that rare breed—an actress/comedian living in Los Angeles.)

The inspiration for my Instagram came to me one afternoon while I was blow-drying a Pekingese named Noodle. Her ears flew up in the air and it was hilarious, so I grabbed my phone and took a video of it. I was so inspired. I started making slo-mo videos every day, of pups majestically blowing in the wind, set to pop music. It was addictive. I remember this amazing moment when the music hit at the exact time Bronson the terrier looked into the camera. I got emotional. It was to a Vacationer song. Now every time I hear that song, I think of him.

I've noticed dogs convey intense and relatable emotion no matter what they're doing. There's never an indifferent look on their face. It's either: *This is the most exciting thing that's ever happened to me in my entire life!!!* or *This is the worst betrayal anyone has ever experienced.* Or, *You're an idiot.* I could take a photo of a dog looking down at a fly on the floor, but if they're all wet and soapy, and I use filters to make the photo a sad blue hue, it looks like this dog is having an existential crisis. Maybe that's why I love expressing myself through these dogs—they're showing vulnerability so I don't have to.

I think dogs mirror our human experience because we project our own truths on to them. Dogs aren't ~~weighed~~ down by politics, gossip, or Twitter (except my poodle, but that's a different book). They don't overanalyze everything. They're pure instinct. They live in the moment. I never gave this any thought until I really looked at all the photos I was taking.

When I first started my business, I wanted to keep it a secret. I didn't even tell people I was a dog groomer. But my little private business kept growing—and my Instagram took off like crazy. It was awesome, and very unexpected, and I can't believe this is my life. My two worlds are colliding now and it's magic.

Can I get hippie-dippie for a sec? *Isn't it funny how when you flow with the universe and just let things happen organically, you vibrate at your highest level?* THAT was gonna be the name of this book but it wouldn't fit on the cover.

Please enjoy *Groomed.*
xoxo,
Jess

The Bath

"You know I know where you sleep, right?"

Punk

Emo

New Wave

Pop

"Today I will manifest abundance."

"Today I will limit crotch sniffing."

"Today I will connect with serenity."

"Today I will let flies live."

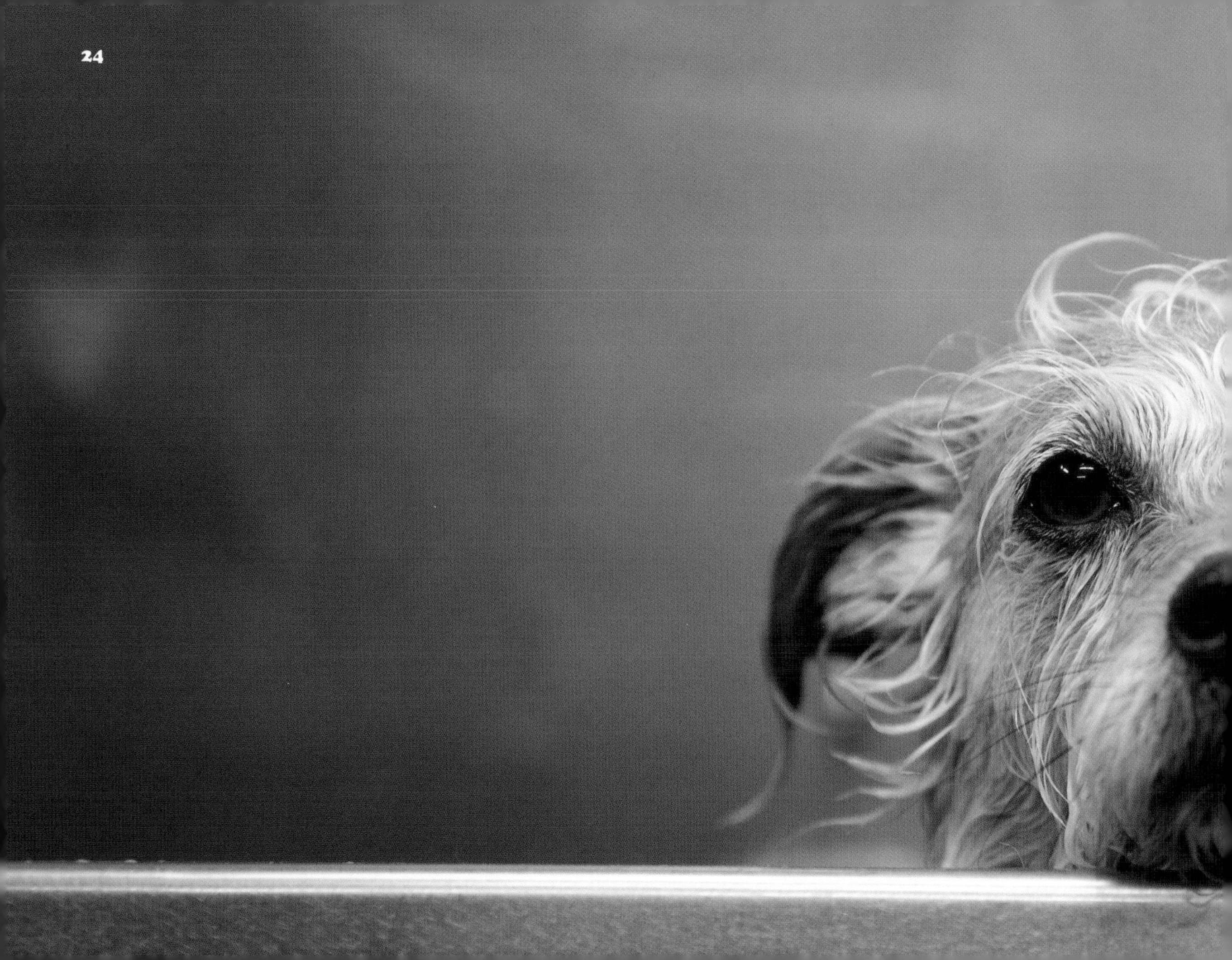

"I think I've hit rock bottom,
but I'm hopeful."

"Is this because I ate a tiny bit of garbage?"

"The caterpillar doesn't question
the breaking point. He accepts it
as fate, and dreams of wings."

"Squirrels. Sprinklers. Peeing. Bones. Chicken liver. Balls . . ."

"I am upset."

"Are you there, god? It's me, Mollie."

"The alarming thing is I didn't even see this coming."

The Blowout

"Even rappers don't flow like this."

John

Paul

Ringo

Schwartz

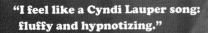

"I feel like a Cyndi Lauper song: fluffy and hypnotizing."

"Flossy, glossy, and saucy, baby."

"The higher the fur,
the closer to god."

"I don't get out of bed for less than ten treats a day."

"Dear haters, picture this
during your morning routine."

"You can't fire me, hunny,
'cause I *quit!*"

"Oh my god, I'm *stunning*."

"My fluff runneth over.
And over."

The Makeover

Olive, Maltese

Likes: artisanal kibble, rope toys, pitching jokes to comedy writers

Dislikes: gardeners, loud things, false connections

Watson, Wheaton Mix

Likes: bully sticks, poetry, *Murder She Wrote*

Dislikes: cats, salesmen, constant inner battles

Bronson, Terrier Mix

Likes: hiking, being organized, heavy metal
Dislikes: garbage trucks, children, Mondays

Butters, Cavalier/Poodle Mix

Likes: chicken, fetch, environmentalism

Dislikes: fireworks, bell peppers, labels

Meemu, Poodle Mix

Likes: car rides, West Elm, his faith

Dislikes: EDM, vegetables, the holidays

Red, Shih Tzu

Likes: ambition, tug of war, Pema Chödrön

Dislikes: pools, lack of blankets, narrow-mindedness

Nugget, (tiny) Poodle

Likes: Joan Crawford docs, pillows, validation

Dislikes: drum machines, negativity, not being held

Scooter, Poodle Mix

Likes: journaling, belly rubs, Bon Jovi

Dislikes: turtlenecks, Labradors, the rain

Penny, Schnauzer Mix

Likes: sunbathing, raw bones, film noir

Dislikes: doorbells, bees, technology

Balki, Havanese

Likes: bike rides, best friends, hats
Dislikes: lizards, beets, fan fiction

Daisy, Poodle

Likes: podcasts, laps, chasing her tail

Dislikes: magicians, being brushed, alarm clocks

Kasia, Yorkie

Likes: giant sequoias, squeaky balls, vintage Chanel

Dislikes: smog, tigers, millennials

Valentina, Maltese

Likes: road trips, pink,
tapping into abundance

Dislikes: bulldogs, the
ocean, trucker hats

Penny, Shih Tzu

Likes: matcha, the *New York Times*, manipulating humans

Dislikes: fragrant candles, extreme heights, being vulnerable

Huckle, Bichon Mix

Likes: agility training, chasing bubbles, improv

Dislikes: yelling, carrots, lack of perspective

Pepper, Havanese

Likes: tiny balls, tiny spaces, large men

Dislikes: spiders, being hungry, political unrest

Pinky, Yorkie

Likes: fuzzy toys, sushi, winning
Dislikes: intolerance, pack rats, plumbers

Pepper, Dandie Dinmont/Poodle Mix

Likes: toy monkeys, burrowing, morning affirmations

Dislikes: being clean, working out, social hierarchies

Pancake, (the tiniest) Poodle

Likes: arguing, scooting, synchronicity

Dislikes: skateboarders, Wayne Newton, social pressures

Josie, Poodle

Likes: cheese, compliments,
running in circles
Dislikes: mice, raisins,
horror movies

The Final Photo Shoot

Behind the Scenes
with Jess Rona

How'd you break into the grooming biz? What inspired you to start your own business?
I started off as a bather when I was nineteen to make some money to buy a car. It was the least "9-5" looking job of the openings listed on the PetSmart application.

It took years to become a business owner, although I've had the entrepreneurial spirit my whole life. I bet I've worked for half the grooming shops in Los Angeles. I've done every job related to grooming, and I always thought "one day when I own my own place, I'll do it my way." I got tired of working for people who weren't groomers themselves and didn't really get it.

I was actually let go from the last shop I worked at and it kind of forced me to finally do my own thing. Getting fired was the best thing that ever happened to me—it changed my life.

What is the most satisfying part of your process?
The most rewarding thing about grooming is the reaction I get from owners when they see their dog after I do a makeover. It's like giving gifts to people every day. I also love when clients let me do a splash of color on a tail or play with a fun style. It keeps my job interesting, and I get to discover new techniques and styles.

If you were a dog, what kind would you be?
A fat poodle.

Is there a particular tool you couldn't live without?
Oooh! My favorites are: Utsumi Half Moon comb; Avanti thinning shears; Cobalt Click Curve shears; and Katana shears. I also love my Wahl cordless clippers and Andis corded clippers, and my Chris Christensen and Artero brushes. It's always fun to try new products and tools, too. There's so much that goes into making a dog gorgeous.

How does music inspire you while you work?
That was kind of how the whole Instagram craze started. I was listening to music and grooming a dog and it was like I was watching a live music video. The song and dog kind of matched in this cool way.

I'm always inspired by music, but there have been moments where music hits me in a deeper way. I remember hearing the song "Fifteen" by Goldroom and it moved me so much. I used it in one of the very first videos I ever made.

I also love listening to audiobooks and podcasts. I just finished *The Alchemist*, the Elena Ferrante novels, and my favorite book ever, *Big Magic* (which I've listened to multiple times). I'm also obsessed with the podcasts *Being Boss*, *You Must Remember This*, *Magic Lessons*, *My Dad Wrote a Porno*, and *The Moth*. I'm a nut.

What's a classic grooming mistake people make when they try to groom their pup at home?
Owners often cut their dog's bangs above the eyes to help them see. But it's the fur between the eyes that makes it hard for a dog to see. (Most groomers are happy to do an in-between bang trim for you.)

The key to making a dog not look like it just lost a fight with a large fan is to cut the hair with the grain (aka, in the direction the hair grows). When you cut with the grain, it blends. When you cut against the grain, it creates a shape (like a weird triangle) you weren't expecting.

What's your top grooming goof of all time?
Oh man, I accidentally dyed a Pomeranian "Smurf" blue when the owner wanted a soft pastel look. Thankfully the owner was super cool and understanding. I felt so badly I went to his house to pick up the dog for free baths for the next few months to try to fade the color.

Do you have a signature style—or favorite furry look?
I love putting my spin on trendy Japanese styles. I call it "Japanese-inspired pet trims." It's a softer take on the whimsical styles popular in Asia.

Why do you think your Instagram (@jessronagrooming) is so popular (and so crazy-loved)?
There's so much darkness in the world and on social media. I think it's a way people can forget about their troubles. It's pure joy.

We filter everything through our own human experience. We are united in that way—because we've all experienced pain and joy. But for some reason if it's expressed by a Shih Tzu, it's hilarious.

Got any tips or tricks you'd like to share with aspiring groomers?
The number one thing I tell new groomers is to be patient. It takes years and years (and years) to get good and comfortable grooming dogs. It's not just the act of grooming a dog, it's learning dog psychology, different skin and coat types, and how to handle difficult dogs and still make them beautiful. Being kind and patient with yourself is the only way to go. Take classes at local trade shows, subscribe to *Groomer to Groomer* magazine, get the *Super Styling Sessions* DVD series by Sue Zecco and Jay Scruggs, enter yourself in a competition, get a subscription to learn2groomdogs.com, watch the pros, and ask questions.

Playlist

The *Groomed* Soundtrack

The Bath	The Blowout	The Makeover	The Final Photo Shoot
Once I Loved by Astrud Gilberto	**Fifteen** by Goldroom	**Come Fly with Me** by Frank Sinatra	**Coffee** by Sylvan Esso
Infinite Arms by Band of Horses	**10,000 Emerald Pools** by BØRNS	**It Was a Good Day** by Ice Cube	**Haunted** by Mr Little Jeans
Gentle Spirit by Jonathan Wilson	**Life's a Dream** by Built to Spill	**Bye Babe** by Lee Hazlewood	**Bam Bam** by Sister Nancy
Blonde on Blonde by Nada Surf	**Do You Realize??** by The Flaming Lips	**Good for You** by Selena Gomez	**Human Nature** by Michael Jackson
I Was a Fool by Tegan and Sara	**I'm 20** by Frankie Cosmos	**Wow** by Beck	**Oh Honey** by Delegation
The Hour by Valerie June	**I Feel It Coming** by The Weeknd	**Good as New** by Vacationer	**Coconut** by Harry Nilsson

Acknowledgments

High fives to Oliver the schnoodle's dad, Jason Rothenberg. Thank you for teaching me how to work a camera, how to organize photos, and for letting me borrow your strobe light knowing full well it would get Pomeranian fluff all over it.

Hugs to Sam and Elaine. Thank you for letting me borrow your fancy camera. You are both tiny and I love you.

Obnoxious bear hug to Shasta Spahn, who was the amazing DP for the flipbook. You are the coolest and I'm so grateful for you.

Endless kisses to Eric ('cause you gotta thank your husband in stuff like this). Thank you forever, baby.

Fist bumps with explosions to my mom, Judith Rona, and my sis, Allison Rona. You have always supported me and helped me when I needed it. Oh, can I borrow $20?

Secret awesome handshakes to Jay and Christine for squeaking squeaky toys and ruffling treat bags like maniacs to get the pups' attention.

Belly rubs to all the dogs in this book. Thank you for letting me take your photo. I'm sure it was annoying for you. To be fair, tons of treats were given.

About the Author

Jess Rona is an actress/comedian/dog groomer. Her Instagram @jessronagrooming, which showcases dogs being blown-dry in slo-mo, all set to catchy pop music, is a bona fide phenomenon. Jess has directed shorts, commercials, and a music video for Tegan and Sara. She's appeared in *New Girl, One Mississippi*, commercials, and lots of web videos. She lives in Los Angeles with her husband and dogs, Chupie and Meemu, and is a notorious over-giver of treats.

Index